GOD is Always There

GOD is Always There

Wherever We Are

John L. Breska

RESOURCE *Publications* • Eugene, Oregon

GOD IS ALWAYS THERE
Wherever We Are

Copyright © 2026 John L. Breska. All rights reserved. Except for brief quotations in critical publications or reviews, no part of this book may be reproduced in any manner without prior written permission from the publisher. Write: Permissions, Wipf and Stock Publishers, 199 W. 8th Ave., Suite 3, Eugene, OR 97401.

Resource Publications
An Imprint of Wipf and Stock Publishers
199 W. 8th Ave., Suite 3
Eugene, OR 97401

www.wipfandstock.com

PAPERBACK ISBN: 979-8-3852-7240-2
HARDCOVER ISBN: 979-8-3852-7241-9
EBOOK ISBN: 979-8-3852-7242-6

VERSION NUMBER 01/22/26

For all who care to lead a peaceful life,
learning along the way, growing in heart and soul.

Contents

Acknowledgment

A warm thank you to my wife, Deborah Breska,
for her artistic touch, which graces this cover.

GOD is Always There

I bow my head to start the day,
a prayer to wash my sins away,
much lighter now in heart and mind,
must never try to be unkind

Improving as I move along,
sweet guidance, knowing right from wrong,
for all the misery out there,
I find there's healing in my prayer

Sometimes I stumble, even fall,
at times I'm hurting, then I call,
for help to ease this troubled man,
GOD's always there, I understand

No clue to what this day will bring,
a soothing salve or sudden sting,
whatever comes to visit me,
my GOD will guide and set me free

A Country Walk

Sometimes I walk the country road to get away from noise,
to listen to creation sing and thus regain my poise,
each bird, a song she calls her own and shares for all to hear,
each chorus from a lofty branch so one can't get too near

The many insects in the fields create their special hum,
as I walk past the corn and hay enjoying sights that come,
the farmer's tractor passes by beneath a partly cloudy sky,
we wave the wave of passing souls in greeting, eye to eye

While walking, I talk on with GOD about the many things,
which cross my mind in silent prayer and hope my prayers have wings,
to rise up in the heavens where the angels have His ear,
that I might live my days in happiness and not in daily fear

The geese are gathering in flocks prepared for a long flight,
I see them just beyond the pond all resting for the night,
the sun is low beyond the trees it's time to turn around
and lest I get lost in the dark, I guess it's homeward bound

Perhaps This Year

Perhaps a prayer to light the way,
a brand–new year, another day,
much guidance in each step we take,
each life, a miracle for what we make
and hope would be we do not break,
along life's varied path

Perhaps a resolution made,
to raise the bar, improve our grade,
for we will walk this path one time,
through weather bad or whether fine,
drink hope, and faith, as a fine wine,
in so, we do the math

Perhaps we start anew this year,
we silence speculative fear
and as a race, we come to grips,
we silence hate from out our lips,
we inner listen for our tips
and soften karma's wrath

Substitute Buddha

What have we learned along the way,
measured work and lengthy play,
dawn brings most another day,
as wisdom often hides

What have we done to help the cause,
time to run and time to pause,
abiding by the karmic laws,
the universe abides

What do we do in the here and now,
answers questions, why and how,
do what you would allow,
where your love resides

Natural Announcement

I love to listen to the wind across a summer field,
it plays a song where crickets do take part
but one must stand still, statuesque, in order for the yield,
for they will stop creation of their art

Tis landscape's symphony you hear, played out beneath the sky,
the melody of life that's in the air,
just listen, and you might get off on Mother Nature's high,
then understand, it needs some extra care

The Helping Man

Our heart breaks for others when they are down,
when tragedy hits and all reason leaves town,
when a soul cries, for life has delivered the news,
in a measure of time, they be deep in the blues

It has happened before, it's been written about,
think we've all had a taste, where we swung and struck out,
but the thing about man, if he carries some good,
we will aid one and other to get out of the wood

And when we are standing, when the tremors subside,
we are grateful I'd hope, for a much calmer ride,
so, we navigate forward 'till the next challenge rears,
believing our neighbors will help comfort our fears

We are passing through places that are unknown at best
and it's our own behaviors that might lengthen the quest,
sad, that sorrow seems destined to bring man to see,
our GOD is alive both in you and in me

Surprise!

It opens one's eyes when you come through the door,
an echoing chant that will rattle your core,
elation of beings shouting glee as they cheer,
in delight, you are shaken, as friends all appear!

Gold for the Soul

Compassion's a trait that's well earned,
for we know what it's like to get burned,
we fathom the grief one can feel,
for we've tasted that unwelcome meal

Its flowers are kindness we share,
warm heart shows another we care,
we pause in today's rapid pace,
to focus our eyes on each face

In living, there's knowledge we find,
if one can be respectful and kind,
there's gold for the soul, so I've heard,
such actions are clear and not blurred

One Given Day (the gift)

Interpretations choirs sing,
about a smile a gift will bring,
when what we say in the exchange,
we searched for joy within your range

We wrap our gifts to one and other,
father, mother, sister, brother
swapping bits of happiness,
in hope, it somehow comes to bless

We, cook great meals this holiday,
we bow our heads, for grace, we pray,
our conscious thoughts of the Lord's birth,
could be, we measure our own worth

For those who celebrate I say,
celebrate GOD each new day,
maybe, our GOD watched over you,
when you were down and thought you through

Could be He moved some other souls,
to help attain your many goals,
perhaps He may, perhaps He might,
guide you on this silent night

Each man is given just one day,
that is GOD's gift, what more to say,
we spend the time, no refunding,
no gifting, for that's not GOD's thing

Who's There

Expression is a flower to one and many
but if a soul lay dormant,
nothing will appear
and yet, the seed within awaits patiently

Enrich your vision, trust in steps forward
and bring the beauty of within,
to the surface of the world, we share
and find your heart is lighter for the fare

Friends

To no other end, a friend,
a special bond which goes beyond,
an ear to share our verbal thought,
about our take on what's been taught

A shoulder when we feel the need,
to grieve, when eyes with tears would bleed,
a happy face that knows our space
and warmth which always leaves a trace

A soul who'll disagree at times
and in life's darkness always shines,
a friend who helps us plant the seed
and reaps the harvest if in need

Sometimes a silent, guiding light,
when we are wounded from a fight,
their spirit seems to know our song,
perhaps that's why we get along

They're gone from harbor to the sea
but most return to share their company,
our friends are gifts each given day
and should be treated in that way

Mortality

I watch the clouds as they drift by
and often I'm to wonder why,
what purpose that I still exist,
for all bad I've done

I hang my head and sometimes sigh,
for times I never seemed to try,
so long, a sad, remorseful list,
I played but rarely won

Seldom did I see eye to eye,
first to party, last to fly,
in my fog or heavy mist,
searching for the sum

Ate my cake and had my pie,
found my feet when not too high,
growing up my folks were mad,
always on the run

Now, the final chapter's nigh,
dare I say, I might could die,
trying hard to get the gist,
why I'm so undone

Quiet Times

At times, I find the quiet in my day,
from the pace of work, beyond the joy of play,
to where distraction loses action
and calm's a centered place along the way,
yet most times, it's a salve that mends my fray

Being Thankful

What purpose being thankful, when it's for another soul,
as it's easy to be thankful when it is our own true goal,
we are thankful when our team does win and takes the trophy home,
are we ok when it goes the other way and sits like a gut stone?

I have come to understand that winning comes in many ways,
it's an abstract lesson hard to see but in greater realms it plays,
when we reach a place where all we are can relate to everything,
I believe it's then, one is rising to, where one hears the angels sing

Now I'm not quite there for the opposition still leaves me in knots
still, I feel I'm on the learning path and great knowledge blooms in spots
but that fact that I've begun to see through the other people's eyes,
seems to startle me in a thankful way and is much to my surprise

If Not for Angels

Affinity for angels I have found,
perhaps that's why I'm still around,
because the Lord is dear to me,
respecting of His infantry

It started with my guardian,
found GOD had legions dear to Him
and I would call, "Protect me Lord,"
in hopes my prayer might send a horde

I've found myself caught in a mess,
throughout this life, I must confess
and when it seemed there was no hope,
the angels came so I might cope

Much gratitude for all those saves,
ninth inning is when this man caves,
I've asked forgiveness of my sins,
while angels stayed, some loss, some wins

So, when you're rescued from great grief
and you are shocked to disbelief,
know there's angels in the wings,
that help with many varied things

The Truth of Innocence

A child sees through children's eyes
and all is inspiration,
the aged see through wisdom's eyes
and thus, comes separation

We sort through evidence to find life's truth
and wonder if it came to us in youth,
we sift the sands through sieve to see,
where truth and lies appear to be

And in our quest to find the light,
some darkness comes within our sight,
for how we could discern the two,
if only one was what we knew

When darkness covers what we see,
we light up our reality,
watch children as they learn their way,
for what they're fed is how they play

Heaven's Gate

We often pray when it's too late,
we see the closing of the gate
and try to slip by silently,
for we are only human

We push and pull our days on earth,
we ponder on our own such worth
and haunted by mortality,
we scramble to be new men

We weep in shadows privately,
we hope there's hope for you and me,
the endgame has us down on knee,
that we are not an orphan

Gate hinges creak as we look on
and wonder when they'll play our song,
in time we come to be set free
and hope we hold a token

Games

I play the game of win or lose but there is more than that,
at times participation seems to be the only fact,
while other times the art of watching is a game as well,
as I cheer on my favorite team until the final bell

It seems that life is quite the game which takes an effort plus,
to do it well for some, while others wonder what's the fuss
but anything they say worth doing is worth doing good,
yet, I did waste life's better part and I'm here, knock on wood

But if inclined to roll the dice and take my lumps as such,
I'd rather have a second chance, I thank you very much,
for there were games I played on everyone including me
and now I wrestle in my sleep with my eternity

November at the Door

November brings us thoughtfulness,
as we sort life's continued mess,
we celebrate our Veterans both present and those gone,
we bow our heads in humble prayer for blessings short and long

It seems to soften up our hearts for special days, December,
as Hanukkah, then Christmas, and Kwanzaa we remember,
perhaps the colder weather has us cozy up unknowing
or gathered in the warmest room where fireplace is glowing

The shoulder chips seem rounded when we hit the grateful season
and love abounds in many hearts for yet, some unknown reason,
I wish it lasted all year long but we all lose our bearing,
a puzzle that is incomplete, that missing piece called caring

A Sign of Peace

The olive branch, a sign of peace,
to rest in better times,
rebuilding all the ruins,
swap the war drums for sweet tunes,
softening the clenched jaw look,
maybe reading the Good book,
finding spring in winter's storm,
where the cold hearts start to warm,
life renewed like seed to earth,
looked upon as the rebirth,
sad, the state we find today,
seems all men have lost their way,
think I'll go and think awhile,
hope to come back with a smile

It's Up to You

Be kind to someone today,
try to have patience and care,
for they might have great problems that we are not aware,
their plate has issues different from ours,
we might chase the rainbow, while they chase the stars

Touch a heart with tenderness
and say a prayer that GOD may bless,
by organizing any mess that haunts a soul today,
look for things that need be done,
do not wait for anyone,
be the start of something new,
which blesses them and shines in you

A To Z

I come to find the quiet more often, so it seems,
for in the silence of my mind, this creature has his dreams,
like entering a library once born of yesterday,
the information index cards appear from A to Z they say

And I am left to scroll through topics which whet the appetite,
for the soul needs stimulation to research the light,
all knowledge, out there, energy, the cloud before the cloud
and only muddled if you will, by darkness as the shroud

That blinds all seekers in this world, embodied endless noise,
so, when I find the quietude, I find I regain poise,
it's much like washing clothes, I've finally come to find,
instead of dirty garments, I'm inclined to clean my mind

Molecules

There's evidence in water that anger changed the cell
and when the cell was frozen it looked to be from hell
and when they spoke of joyous things the cells took on a form,
that sparkled like the Christmas star, though cold, the image warm

So, when they tell you talk to plants and even, maybe sing,
tis beauty which will start to grow, then flowers, plants will bring,
it gives one pause to mark our actions in the positive,
for it will have a great effect on just how well we live

Hole in the Choir

There's a hole in the choir where voice use to be,
like the forest who wonders of the missing tree,
even though all the others try to fill in the breach,
there's an octave still missing that the rest cannot reach

Though she sings in the heavens with angelic ties,
when her notes are without, sadness fills our eyes,
choir practice is lacking her infectious laugh
and the route she walked home on, is an empty path

All will sing with their choir in eternity,
nothing short in the forest will we ever see
and our hearts will not grieve for an empty chair,
for our song will sing on though she's no longer there

At What Length, Truth

If the measure of a man be truth
and two men find in their search,
that they reach different conclusions,
where does the sum of their equation rest,
for in absolutes, the finality must be in reality
and not in the minds of thinkers,
for perception would most likely be,
thumb on scale or the baker's dozen,
which often finds one short at the end of the day

Tailoring

We measure the cloth of the day,
then cut and stitch away,
taking the fabric
and creating what we wear,
through those hours,
what we share,
that we care,
that we remain time aware

We are the tailors of our lives,
fitting the garment of the hour,
we sew what's in our power
and make the alterations as we go,
our hope is that we clothe our being so,
not for splendor nor for show,
but for the trip we can't forego

A Stone's Throw

I throw a stone,
you throw a stone,
in truth, we've given each, a new home,
one thousand years pass
and there sit the stones,
whereas we, at best, are a pile of bones

Those bones leave little clues behind,
diet, age, and wounds they find
but they won't know our football team,
party affiliation, or how we dream,
they won't even know the stones we threw
both at me and me at you

Young Ahab

Mist over early morning waters,
splashes heard but still unseen,
rowboat cuts the liquid like a falcon slices air,
as I make my way toward visions in my mind,
of elusive, great fish, who toys with my expectations

Stealth as a young boy checking out the Christmas bounty,
I move closer to the ultimate spot,
wind has not awakened,
so, I drift over what I deem as the X upon the water

I cast, listening to the line peel away,
then the contact of lure breaking the surface,
in my mind it drifts downward fifteen feet,
as I begin the task of reeling in with sporadic precision
and the hope of a strike

Grateful to Be Humble

Humility is a sea traversed with torn and tattered sails,
in a ship without a rudder,
through storms of great magnitude,
still finding land without a sextant,
dashed against the rocks,
only to awaken on the shore,
tired but unscathed

Into This World

Small wonder,
a child born of innocence,
tame or wild,
something, in the nature of us all,
named but not defined,
for new titles need to search and find,
just who we truly are,
whether down to earth or a shooting star

Penny Ugly

We found an ugly penny that had surely seen its day,
"Ninety–nine more, a dollar," Dad would always say,
I wondered of its travels from mint to who knows where
and if it had some tales to tell if it could only share

I guess I've seen a bunch of them as I moved on through time,
passing thoughts remind me there were nickels and a dime,
that penny had a weathered look like life out on the street
and years had passed since it had shined when minting was complete

We all have been that penny as we traversed through our lives,
good times were grand upon this land, while bad times brought out hives
and later years we found the soap, we polished up our act,
face value changed and thus our worth and brother, that's a fact

So, if you find a penny, pick it up for life moves fast,
remember you were once brand new in the not so distant past,
then think of those around you, as you clean up and you shine,
to let them know the Minter loves and many still have time

And Then You'll Be Happy

The value of a precious stone exists if there's a buyer
and so, we set our many wants up with each man's desire,
they sell it to us with the notion we will be much better,
like flood insurance for the guy who grew up a bed wetter,
they suck us in, to take a ride,
selling us some phony pride,
instead of grooming what's inside,
to earn the heart its letter

The Clarity of Knowledge

Depth of water has its merits,
for shallow puddles always muddle any clarity,
by clouding up what once was there
and when distance to the bottom,
is increased, we tend to see,
that which lies beneath reality,
while further evidence would show,
that when the quest is far below,
we seldom know the bliss,
for unbeknownst to us,
the answer hides in the abyss,
perhaps because discovery,
eludes the seeker's curiosity

All the Time

On every compass should be etched,
a positive direction, a path so blessed,
for threads which hold society together,
fray away it seems to me, in the best of weather
but I find when storms approach,
we need no coach,
to find our hearts when we're in need
and each soul helps with a good deed

We rise up in calamity,
to fix the ship when lost at sea,
salvation both for you and me
but where's the hand when we reach land,
we fade like smoke on last night's fire,
smoldering, with no desire

The pendulum swings both to and fro,
I guess that's karma's stop and go,
what little that I swear I know,
it would be fine if we might show,
our love all of the time

The Stray (for Colleen)

Imagine the nightmare of a homeless dog,
who wanders the earth like a hair on frog,
there are no set meals nor trips to the Vet,
there's never the moniker that this is a pet

But rather a scavenger looking for food,
chased away, shot at, or cursed, which is rude,
they sleep where they might, find a moment of rest
but more times than not they are skittish at best

They growl out of fear for they have lost their trust,
they stay on the edge for survival's a must
and sadly, the guilty ones never are caught,
they release the dog who should never been bought

Or they tend to let over breeding take place
and let some run free, for they've run out of space,
the problem is ill–advised humans at best,
abuse and plain ignorance, sprawled on their chest

How sad that man's best friend, is treated so low
but it's happening now, and I thought you should know!

Chinese Fortune Cookie

It seems like only yesterday I wondered of tomorrow
and if it would be filled with joy or a day of sorrow,
maybe somewhere in between, where balance finds an even place,
a smile and a chortle or a teary frown upon this face,
we never know what cards we're dealt, until we get the hand,
we know not how the song is played, until we hear the band
and we won't ever fall unless we try to rise and stand

Time Share

They say the novelty wears off,
the things that trend all find their end,
that yesterdays are novelties of memories
and we are simply passing through

So, if at all, these words are true,
should the likes of me and you,
find our common ground,
enjoying life while we're around,
treating everything we touch,
with respect and love, so much,
we dissipate the rising hate,
which overboils as of late
or maybe has since GOD knows when

Talk sweet to plants and everything,
make the atoms start to sing,
life could be a better thing,
Amen!

Autumn Introductions

The gathering of birds is the introduction to autumn,
whereas weeks prior, they all went their separate ways
and now find comfort in the numbers of their species,
difference between a solo or an orchestrated piece,
for now, they dance the air in like rhythm,
much as concert goers sway to the recognizable tune

Soon tall fields will be shorn,
while deer and turkey will pick at the rubble,
great orange pumpkins, along with green and yellow gourds,
will fill the farmer's wagon as he tractors his yield in from field

Cool nights ahead with crisp, sunny days,
leaves drop from trees, preparing the way,
fall football, color changes, and gathering,
preparation for cold winter days,
snowy, early morning sounds of muffled shovels over sidewalks,
a time for fireplaces, novel reading, and bake goods,
bird feeders, thankful holidays, along with spiritual reflection

But for now, we watch the colors light the autumn trees,
enjoy fresh smells of soups on stoves,
fresh air fills our lungs, as we move through pleasant days,
enjoying gifts, we sometimes overlook at times,
too preoccupied, for life gets in our way,
I've heard them say!

Wishing Well

I dreamt there was a bucket in an empty wishing well
and when I drew the vessel up, it was dry like Dante's hell,
I made a wish with hands in prayer, for the water that should be,
at the bottom of the endless hole that had echoed uselessly

Then I lowered down the bucket on the worn and tattered rope,
with each turn I cranked, it moved from sight, but I found that I had hope,
as the world was hot and parched these days and man's temper burst to flame,
thoughts of quenching mankind came to mind, thus cooling down the blame

I thought I heard a distant splash as I waited for a time,
then I turned the crank and slack, feeling weight, a pleasant sign,
well, the journey seemed to last forever in recovering the gift
but I eyed the liquid just below, hoisting bucket with a lift

I took the wooden ladle and I scooped it carefully
and I brought it toward my lips but stopped, as a tear fell out of me
while I thought of all who thirst, for that which would give their soul some peace
and the fire burning deep inside fueling anger might just cease

Wanderers

Back in nineteen sixty–one I walked the railroad tracks,
Milwaukee Road was my abode, where hoboes toted sacks,
we wandered on, my comrades, where the rails had no end,
if just to see what came to be, by going 'round the bend

Peter, Pat, and Carl too, seem whom I recollect
and if I've overlooked a soul, regrets, with great respect,
the visions blur as time pulls on but those were such good times,
the gully, tracks, and freight trains yes, and the railroad signs

Heading Home

So many versions of GOD's plan,
confuses almost every man,
a quest that's hidden in plain sight,
the difference of both, dark and light

We seldom call when life is grand
but often when we need a hand
and yet, there's always time for us,
when overwhelmed, we tend to fuss

In all the corners of the world,
great words are written then unfurled,
a guide to where to find and seek,
we wait the line, for all are meek

Interpretation is the foe,
for men both push and men both tow,
we make the best of what we find,
above all else to love, be kind

We lose our way throughout our days
and he who's lost is he who prays,
great comfort in we're not alone,
for all involved are heading home

Release

Can't seem to find my dog today,
a week ago, he went away,
my heart tells of a better place,
where all dogs find their special space

Where children come to play with them,
where laughter reigns and joy's a gem,
where life continues on, pain free,
they wait, I'm told, for you and me

I hear his bark throughout the day
and hurt inside, my selfish way,
his eyes told us to please let go,
and so, we did, we loved him so

My tough guy stance collapsed that morn,
he said goodbye, to touch still warm,
no words I know can ever say,
how hard it was that past Monday

Early Morning Preamble

Dawn approaches like a ship in the night,
sails low, as she glides upon the waters,
hull cuts the blackness as she draws near,
bringing much needed light,
for the world fears the darkness,
as well as the creatures who slip through the shadows,
working negative energies about the land

All hope for peace
but there is much work to be molded,
into values which rise above,
the banks of failed oceans of promise

I look to the waters in wait
and realize the many who stand along the shore,
sharing in the anticipation

Benched

Observations from the park bench,
fill my eyes with images, of people on the move,
some are young and pushing strollers,
runners catching up to something

Others waiting for them up ahead,
seniors, some with canes or walkers,
following the path,
toddlers crying for attention,
in their tiny world, such wrath!

Songbirds sing sweet melodies,
dancing on the summer breeze,
gray squirrels dart about the park,
up and on, between the trees

There's an old man turning pages,
book in hand, deep in thought,
young couple laughs and giggles,
as they do the mating dance

Time to rise up from my viewpoint,
for my stay to rent has passed
and someone new might sit a spell
to watch the world move by,
a living canvas 'neath the sky

Life's Lessons

Nothing but the what and where wait outside the door,
for the why is unexplained until we ask for more,
information starts to build upon the steps we take,
toward answers undiscovered as the sleeper stirs, awake

Through rain and sleet, we trek about for the hidden key,
clues are given to the searchers, much like you and me,
as we try to grasp the legend written on the map's last page,
we end up somewhat puzzled, as in time we quickly age

You'd think we'd get there sooner but distraction leaves us lost
and when in dire straits, we'll pay the price no matter cost,
if only we had followed all the clues upon the map,
perhaps we'd never fallen into such a noted trap

We try to guide our children but they haven't got the ears,
in time there's understanding, at the cost of many tears
and so, it is and so it goes, because it's always been,
it comes to all in their own time and only GOD knows when

Throwing in the Towel

Destination of a towel on the shelf inside a store,
purchased for the bathroom as a means to get a body dry,
color coordinated to the paint and to, so much more,
over time, it earns its keep by hanging on the wall,
decorative to the theme, to catch the viewer's eye

Soon it is replaced for looks and put to daily use,
it dries, then finds biweekly wash for sour's no excuse,
then once more, it's dried again,
folded for the linen closet, used when who knows when

The color fades, the edges fray
and time comes when it's thrown away,
turned into some quarter cuts of cloth another day
and finds a home in the garage, next to the shopping bags,
a spot that all the household knows, is where we keep the rags

We all have journeys so to speak,
we start out grand and end up meek
but we maintain purpose in the roles we play,
always looking to be useful for another day

Serious Jokes

The serious side to comedy is its timing after all,
delivering the punchline or taking a prat fall,
we've all been there to tell story or a tale or two,
then forgot the closing line and look like just a fool

Reminds me of the prison where numbers were the jokes
and when somebody shouted out a number to those blokes,
they'd visualize the story then laugh themselves to sleep,
a part of their long sentence in the BIG house, for their keep

A Conundrum

Great reserve the cactus has while waiting on the rain,
standing tall in desert lands, a still life on the plain,
home for the Gila Woodpecker safe among the spines,
Saguaro flowers, nectar, for the hummingbirds at times

All things, a commitment for each other's wellbeing,
only takes the searching eyes to understand the seeing,
each living thing, a puzzle piece of something greater,
when taken away, only leaves life's cycle with a crater

The General Store

A bit of this and that, fills up the many shelves and nooks,
a poultice for infected wounds, some catalogs, and books,
canned fruit, dried cereal, and feed for horses, by the sack,
plus, nails in the barrel or lumber in a stack out back

Writing paper near the ink, hard candy for the girls and boys,
a hammer, square, and ball of string, and even a few toys,
there's colored fabric just beyond the old woodstove, aglow
and lengths of rope for mule or packhorse loaded up in tow

Coffee and a flour sack, some hardtack, matches, bullets too,
for the boots, some saddle soap, a tin of chew, and that should do,
a couple apples for the horse and one small map to guide,
a fella heading way out west to find a place that ain't been tried

Man on a Raft

Few signs of peace on the horizon
and yet, I'm a believer,
that man can overcome his ego,
humble himself to an understanding,
that we all rent our time upon the earth
and though we have some differences,
those anomalies are but a drop,
within an ocean of familiarity that we share

Independence Day

Our independence founded, that it is in GOD we trust,
all men created equal is another given must,
life, liberty, and pursuit of happiness, come to mind,
we have asked for nothing more nor less I find

And yet there lives a cancer rooted deep within the land,
which takes a knee defiant of those patriots that stand,
when there are other platforms to air disagreements out,
where representatives can do more than to lie or pout

No truth in moving forward on the way to destruction,
no peace in just ignoring truth, to get a new election,
we try our best to understanding social arguments,
we try to balance liberty, our lives, and make some sense

Our flag, a symbol of Americans who passed this way before us,
our song's verses written strong with two–line chorus,
brings honor to creation of this Country's love and worth,
going back to when our Founding Fathers gave it birth

Unsolved Mysteries

We look to unsolved mysteries for clues that mark the way,
for answers sometimes hidden are found in light of day,
while others hide in shadows, which live throughout the night
and seem to hold us prisoners while measuring our fright

But truth cannot be altered nor tainted by a lie,
it only lives as truth, for it was born, so it will die
and even then, it is not changed into a synonym,
it stays a truth, an honesty, by word or put to hymn

While mysteries are sometimes solved by measuring the truth,
unraveled like the ancient scroll that opens for the sleuth
and there inside the message although old, it plainly reads,
one cannot grow unless we take to task, to plant the seeds

Many Things

Getting past the reasoning of owning many things,
that happiness is not so measured by the joy it brings,
for something new does quickly fade to boredom in our wealth
and we are most obliged when ill, to contemplate good health

One takes the time to recollect when life had uphill struggle
and we had trouble breaking free from years stuck in a bubble
but then prosperity came knocking on our own front door
and we began accumulating just a wee bit more

Salvation Army, Goodwill, and a rummage sale or two,
balance out the stash of things we finally outgrew
and as we age, we find we carry simply less and less,
for simplicity we find, creates a lesser mess

Ingredients

The depth of understanding could give some of us the bends,
for the knowing's in the rowing which the action often lends,
to finding out the meaning behind what was so implied,
was there substance to the process or was everyone denied

Were assumptions mere theatrics on the universal stage
or did footnotes try explaining at the bottom of the page,
were we left to inspiration or a whimsical lament,
was the author so delighted as to sign the work's cement

In the recipe quite hidden there are hints within the dish,
as the flavor's subtle seepage meets the taste buds with a wish,
that participation in the act can often tell the tale
but ingredients have always saw the lesson far from fail

Runners (for David Howey)

The runner always seems content with only just one goal,
that he can reach it sooner than the rest
and if no competition then the time becomes the toll
and it's up to him to try to beat his best

I watch them pass my window as I contemplate the day,
they move from right to left or left to right,
I'd ask them where they're headed but they always run away,
from dawn until the day has turned to night

Still, I Wonder

Lately I've been thinking overtime,
watch the sky while birds fly by,
wonder where they come and go,
wonder if they even know

I wonder if the rain willstop
or if they'll ever plant the crop,
if global showers drown the flowers
and if we're planting more cell towers

It's crossed my mind, it's hard to find,
a dozen people who are kind
and who on earth would skip a place,
where a long line had been the case

I see society erode,
the other day I saw a toad,
he looked at me and I looked back,
we went our way without attack

I wonder if I'm wasting time,
wondering the reason why,
or might I simply find my way,
instead of watching birds all day

Time to Change Horses

Challenges of life are many and few,
some are for me, while others for you,
we each have a road to travel life on
and shortcuts add miles beneath the hot sun,
we're tested in order to see the light,
we're taught the same action,
won't get any traction,
most difficult, drowning, a person can't win,
lost, they go under, unable to swim

The view is the same when you're down on the ground,
so, rise to the challenge but don't groan a sound,
self-evidence comes when self-pity is gone
and we have the chance then to write our own song,
the road has its ups and its terrible downs,
while wisdom comes late, past the many ghost towns,
those places bad choices evicted our dreams
but hard work will build a small city it seems

Inspiration

We wait at times for inspiration to knock upon our door
and find there's only silence for a time and maybe more,
we hope some great idea will fill the void perceived,
we think on things much harder and are never quite relieved

Then as a great tsunami, we are overwhelmed with thought,
ideas flood us endlessly, that before, could not be bought,
from desert to a garden, we have flipflopped in a blink
but take no credit or byline which enabled one to think

I'm much inclined to thank the Lord for His opening the gate,
perceiving that I got there early or I was too late,
the flow returns as moving water in a mountain stream,
as I begin to write it down in the context of my dream

Our Colors

One nation stands beside its colors,
flowing freely in the wind,
reminding one of our foundation,
built with great determination,
striving for a creed of honor,
among the clouds and sky,
fighting for all people, far and nigh,
forever grateful to the fallen,
to the living who endeavored,
to the active fight for freedom,
our colors held forever high

Tomorrow

We look to tomorrow,
when today has just begun
and miss out on the moments,
like pearls tossed in the ocean,
then soon the fading sun

Tomorrow begins,
while we lean into the future,
never knowing if we are in the plan,
if there is a table setting guaranteed,
so, we should digest what we can,
look deep into the flower,
to understand the seed,
know our place in time
and what we truly need

The American Indian

Indigenous spirits please forgive,
we left one place that we may live
but in our zealousness, we stood,
to wipe out all of you we could,
so, we might find a better life,
we cut you down with gun and knife,
we took away your dignity,
that we could prosper and be free,
we drove you out across this land,
wrote treaties that would never stand,
for our ancestors, their poor ways,
forgive, for karma haunts our days

In the Northern Land

There's a cabin in the woods that's been lost to nature's time
and it sleeps the sleep of yesterdays, when the place was new and fine,
rusted axe still stuck in the stump, where the owner split a cord,
wildflowers growing just inside, through a rotted floorboard

Nests have graced the eves in early spring, through the broken window's glass,
while loons who cruise out on the lake call the fauna all to mass,
moss grows vibrant green on the shaded roof, which is weathered from the years,
while the red squirrel chatters from on high just explaining all his fears

Pinecones find their way to the forest floor, in the silence of the day,
as the waves lap on the pier and shore, just a couple casts away,
once the children ran 'round the cabin's land, where adventures came to be,
at times they saw a doe and fawn in the clearing, near the large pine tree

In the great Midwest, in the northern land, where the rivers flow through lakes,
was a place I knew, where the ground squirrels played, where man's spirit slowly wakes,
where the muskellunge moved beneath the waves and the black bear owned land,
where the northern lights would dance on the sky, as we heard the cricket band

A Reason to Learn

Flowers reaching toward the sky,
remind me of the when and why,
we plant the seeds which come to bloom,
we write the notes to some new tune,
we look to possibilities,
while some are small as snowdrops
and others tower, like oak trees,
then through it all we tend to grow,
blossoming for what we know,
not for grandeur nor for show
but for reason in life's season

The Answers Are Tender

Know my heart, not my skin,
know the values deep within,
know the song of my soul,
know that peace is my goal

Know, that we all leave a trail,
full of hurts which make us frail
and the truth in our being,
are the faults we are seeing

Not outside of our essence,
for in time, we're senescence
but the energy we are,
we are near and afar

Know the life we are growing,
in the love which we are showing,
know the answers are tender,
that the warm heart will render

The Rose

Behold the rose in nature's pose,
illuminated color, aided by the sun,
stem of thorns protecting one,
flower petals spread in awe,
warms a heart by what eyes saw,
soon the petals fall to earth,
as a new bud starts to form,
varied names one would suppose,
to the audience at hand, a rose

Warmer Observations

The trees are filling in with leaves,
somewhere flowers breaking ground,
winter hides away and grieves,
a silent mourn, without a sound

The warmer air flows through our hair,
as we dance the dance of spring,
life seems open, without care,
birds are singing on the wing

Boats are back out on the lakes,
sunblock prices start to soar,
thatching lawns with rusty rakes,
lawn chairs out and so much more

Makes a soul feel much alive,
appreciating life and such,
little things which give us drive,
like a newborn baby's touch

A Lesser Time to Dream

Would we be kinder souls,
if a count of days remaining,
would be handed out
or would we argue,
they were given more than me,
so, where's the true equality
or would we draw from Mercy's stream
and open up our hearts,
to those with less a count than me,
a lesser time to dream

The Drifter

I walked with curiosity, the alleys and the streets,
as some new explorer in search of some great treasure,
past stop signs, traffic lights, and stores that carried treats,
finding some things not so good, while others brought me pleasure

Some days, I had companions as adventures would unfold,
the well of curiosity kept us stretching boundaries,
still, we had our limits for we were not very old,
as we grew in adolescence we expanded like the trees

We'd trek downtown to see some girl who had a part time job
or to County Stadium to see Milwaukee's Braves
or a walk to the State Fair to get corn on the cob,
cutting through the Veterans Cemetery, oh, so many graves!

We came upon both rivers and some winding streams,
sat beside the waters, tossing stones, and thoughtful sharing,
about the stuff that mattered and our sorted dreams,
then moved on to discover something quite a bit more daring

I feel I had a childhood that sparkled in a way,
full of great discoveries which educated me,
I made a few wrong turns I'd say, but came out just OK,
I even had some time to watch Roy Rogers on TV

Whisper in a Noisy World

Go quietly,
be mindful of your pace,
be light that filters through the trees,
gently, with great ease,
as not to ripple water
nor push against the wind
or fight the one who guides you,
beneath a hue of blue

And keep in mind your end goal,
make sure your heart is true,
for charting destinations is the start of finding you,
then when you've found the handle,
open up the door,
for where you found beginnings,
is the start of so much more

Resurrection 101

Rise internally like the Easter lily toward the light,
rest in the warmth of all that guides us through the night,
seek joy and understanding, that we all are fragile flowers,
move darkness from our hearts through our remaining hours

Wash forevermore man's old sorrows, weighing down the meaning,
step outside for all those moments you have but been dreaming,
the key to breaking free from chains which bind us all from growing,
is one who's known as love, who guides the boat that we are rowing

This Place

A place I go for quiet time has seemed to disappear,
for now, I cannot find my roost although it was quite near,
a sanctuary all my own to wash my soul each day,
has either disappeared you see, or have I lost my way

Deep in my heart and mind, it waits for me to find the key,
it is a place that's tranquil, where my spirit longs to be,
that centered place behind this face you all have come to know,
is where I go to, when I feel, I've drifted from GOD's glow

I water me with better thoughts of kindness as I be,
then slowly grow up toward the light, much like the old oak tree
and as I stand out in this noise, I come to find GOD's grace,
unlock the door, at least for now and be here, in this place

Just Winging It

Much to learn from watching birds,
they always sing their chosen words,
they make their nests to have their chicks,
from grasses and the finest sticks

They rise before the crack of dawn
and always greet the day with song,
they fly about the world with grace,
yet, somehow always know their place

Each species given certain traits,
yet, seldom ever deviates,
they know their place, they know their song
they even know to get along

Under the Big Top

Small wonder, man on earth,
I muse if GOD finds worth,
to keep the circus one more year,
for clowns might wander far and near

Dark thunder and I bow,
humbled then and even now,
deep down, somehow, I wish I knew,
if I'd be flopping one clown shoe

Calliope on ear,
sawdust underfoot, I fear,
the way we work, like Big Top acts,
our lives in circles, that's the facts

Might try to find yourself,
get yourself up off the shelf,
we all are there, performers strong,
we too, have sung the circus song

To Turn the Page

Owl calls past twilight time to say,
farewell the day,
a mournful song with wide eyed look,
to close the chapter of the book,
to turn the page from light to night,
where many wait the dawn
and while nocturnal creatures roam,
there's countless deep, asleep at home,
the two sides to one's life it seems,
keeps moving while the other dreams

Clean Sweep

There's a spiritual understanding about cleaning,
as we tidy up around our place,
leaving less than any trace,
that we were here and there, leaving piles of debris,
creating a less pleasantry,
like mud upon our face, in the bubble that we pace

And as without we are within,
considering the world we make,
that what we give remains our stake,
in sharing of the way
and though we're only passing through,
the less the hoarder we become,
the brighter is the day

When We Lose Someone

We are left with memories to cling to,
most positive times meet a comforting way,
as an emptiness rings this day true,
we are given hope by our friends, encouragement each day

We are lost within ourselves for mourning,
slow motion unfolds as grief comes to stay,
it heals the body's trauma in the dawning,
over time's long trail, we begin to heal in our own way

A Life in the Day

We search the world over for understanding at best,
we look at our existence as a hunger that won't rest,
we find a moment here and there, where life appears and smiles,
then search the many days and hours across so many miles

We find a day when quiet comes, to sit at twilight time,
while mauves and oranges dance the sky, a truly peaceful sign,
we watch, as slowly stars appear, as nighttime comes to rest
and know we are alive with love, for love is in our nest

Then turmoil strikes and we are scattered farther than our thought,
as we take in the great chagrin, more than what we have bought,
adjustments made, the raging sea finds time and place to calm
and we survive another day as time moves slowly on

My Mother

Of all the mothers in the world I have one that is mine,
breech birth brought me in this life, Aquarian, my sign,
she guided me, though I fell short, for I knew more than she
and though I bumped my head through life she always has loved me

She's ninety–four and still remembers all the grief I churned,
remembers all the rivers crossed and bridges that I burned,
she's not as active as she was, a whirlwind in her day
but ask her on those memories and she can guide the way

She lost her mother very young, before she reached her teens
and though she never mentions it, I'm sure it dashed her dreams,
so, while she's here I let her know, with kisses and a grin
that I am still her baby boy who started out within

The Tougher Side to Love

We're born away to life and more,
we pass through time and each new door,
we know the separation comes,
to all who ever were
but when a soul returns to GOD,
us mourners weep while feeling odd,
the hole inside our heart is wide,
tears pour for someone else has died

Judgement Day

I sat down near the riverbank then watched the water flow
and wondered on tomorrow thinking, GOD might let me know,
if all I ever brought to mind, might be destroyed in future days,
this land we call America, dismantled of its ways

A cancer fouled the waters, and the fish were belly up,
I saw what we had fought for, now, a dried out, empty cup,
for chaos came to dinner and insanity took hold,
destruction was the mantra and their eyes were icy cold

Most networks spun a story that our country hated blacks
but when you saw statistics, this was way far from the facts,
perps became the martyrs and the cops were shot on sight,
this bloodshed bold in daylight, what was once a crime at night

The narrative was evil, twisted words without real facts,
dark money fueled the fire and the flood of violent acts,
tried narratives beyond the pale to remove the President,
with money from our citizens which was constantly ill spent

There's blood within the waters of the river that I see,
the blood of many warriors who did keep our country free,
remains a person's duty to fight for truth's own way,
I know I'll vote for Freedom when it comes to judgement day

The Collective

Visions that these eyes have seen,
sometimes cow, sometimes the cream,
places where this body's been,
long forgotten stops back then

Smiles and frowns were taken in,
losses, ties, a timely win,
black and white and color too,
ground that passed by shoe from shoe

Central Park from way up high,
Lennon died, where fans did cry,
mountains in the eastern north,
great parades on July fourth

Nuns in grade school, watching me,
at Class Clown Academy,
saintly as a choirboy,
summers free, a total joy

Many sights have passed these eyes,
some, I cried, to my surprise,
people here and now, some gone,
seems they heard a shorter song

Memories all stacked inside,
of the many things I've eyed,
wonder what next, I might see,
dawn or GOD's eternity

Wisdom That Is Granted

A longer journey growing old, I often thought to be
but now I find I'm getting nearer by the things I see,
those items that are on the floor seem far away today,
while I approach them with more science as I bend and sway

I used to take long walks and ponder on this life of mine
but now a journey for the mail seems to be just fine,
I stare at wrinkles on my hands then wonder of the cause,
remembering the things accomplished, gives a man real pause

I look at children like they're acorns prior to tall oaks,
I understand the pain I caused to my endearing folks,
wisdom's often granted to the ancient man, I guess,
as he looks to yesterdays to keep from making the same mess

I'm still alive through creaks and groans with alternating pain
and I'll outguess the weatherman when sunshine turns to rain,
I never wear a watch you know, yet conscious of the time
and I awoke this latest dawn, so I'm still doing fine

Keeping the Faith

A sadness in my heart today,
I find my knees and I start to pray,
for in one year our country's died,
they killed small business or have tried

They trampled on our deep belief
and left our world without relief,
as politicians played their game,
they hurt mankind while they would reign

They told us what to do each day
and broke their rules, so they could play,
takes everything to keep my peace,
while they continue with their fleece

This time of year, we mark the birth,
of Jesus Christ and our own worth,
within our hearts, we find our way
and hope we see a better day

It seems that only money talks,
while government, both chokes and balks,
but in our faith, we find the light,
each given day and silent night

So be of gracious heart dear friend
and understand there is no end,
for GOD has plans we cannot see,
that stretch for all eternity

The Way Through Life

See me in the shadows cast from mountains great,
see me in the river as it winds throughout the glen,
see me in the hawk who rides the currents high,
watch me as I live and die

See me where the deer run free in forests green,
see me where the trout hide out in those deeper pools,
see me where the turkeys feed in open fields nigh,
watch me as I live and die

See me under thunder clouds as rain washes the earth,
see me under wood and rock as insects work the land,
see me under bright clear skies that shine on down from sky,
watch me as I live and die

See me on the streets we walk as faces tell the tale,
see me on pews at church where faith is called upon,
see me on the way through life as I go passing by,
watch me as I live and die

Passing Through

The puzzle's answer eludes us,
as we burn calories trying to crack the safe,
still, some things will not answer to a simple question
and remain a mystery,
leaving open chapters in the thinker's mind

We will leave behind treasure we have never seen,
quests incomplete,
places we have heard of, yet unseen to one and all
but for the time we shared and the moments we weaved,
alone or with another,
our imprint on the earth will fade with man
but GOD will not forget

Life's Melody

The finger dance on ivory,
sends ears the haunting melody,
of life, of death, of in between
and spirit moves to the unseen

The notes pour out upon the day,
we tap our toes along the way,
sadness comes then happiness,
each day quite full for nonetheless

The gentle tap upon the keys,
is life, when life is just a breeze,
the heavy handedness at times,
plays apocalyptic signs

One tune subsides, another plays,
so, life goes on its many days,
an ode to keys, both black and white,
much like each one, both day and night

When fingers rest and day has gone,
wish I danced more with my song,
still hear those notes play at my door,
I'll listen on till there is no more

I've Learned to Pray

Of all the gifts that come my way,
the gift of life lights up my day,
for when I wake before the dawn,
I say my prayers then travel on

I hope my day is filled with joy,
like when I was a little boy,
but if a challenge comes to stay,
I'll never let it block my way

A puzzle solver I will be
and search until I find the key,
I'll wear a smile upon my face,
to add than take away my grace

And when they ask me how I cope,
I'll share that I renew my hope,
each morning when I meet the day,
I'm thankful, that I've learned to pray

The Fortunate Man

Light breaks the window,
like the gentle spotlight of a stage,
as she fingers her hair,
in a way that one daydreams,
soft are her eyes
and her mouth muses of some happiness,
she is content in the moment,
I dare not make a sound as I observe,
clouds separate the rays,
which dance upon her skin,
her mind is somewhere beyond the room,
at a time when the fruit was sweet,
and love was an aspiring oak,
strong in the winds of adversity,
and comforting in the August shade,
in her, the girl now a woman,
who's found herself,
and I am the fortunate man

I Know Not When

Found pieces of me missing,
as I looked toward yesterday,
the further I looked back,
the less there was, I'd say

Quiet tune at the moon,
as I went wondering by,
did I really live those years,
I moaned, beneath a sigh

With progress we gain footing,
move on through wisdom's trail,
missed great lessons looking back,
as I searched for my own tail

Say, every day's a journey,
as I wonder where I sail,
suggestions guide the way
but each step forth, I do pale

Less steps remain, I venture,
than the miles that have been
but I will keep on moving,
up until I know not when

Solving the Lesson

The truth about learning,
is the hunger and yearning,
to know the why in understanding,
what defines an answer to the question,
leaving one satisfied,
that their thirst quenched,
they can move on to the next conundrum,
only hoping that all the pieces come together,
pray nothing's missing,
creating a hole and incompletion,
to a passing grade

He's Always Home

When edges of your sanity fray
and you hope the threads will simply go away,
then you watch the clock, like a certain time,
will strike, then everything be fine

When those things you put in order, do not stay
and your world is more than not, in disarray,
when you panic that the end is near,
know there's no substance for your fear

When life burns like a quickened fuse
and you feel you're simply out of dues,
remember always, there's another way,
an understanding of the day

When you cannot fill the glass half full,
when you tire of the endless bull,
you are never, ever, all alone,
just call on GOD, He's always home

The Awakening

Friend and family drop like leaves from my living tree,
moving on to the spirit realm where peace reigns
and love is the norm of each and everyone
but for now, I shall stay with those who remain
and work on loving all, today,
for tomorrow holds the secrets of what will come,
while life's dance moves with music of the hour

Lessons in learning who we were
and who we are today,
are still available to the seekers in this life
and I am but a student of the awakening,
a stone in the stream of existence,
polished over time

The Loss of Freedom

I dreamt I found an open grave and looked down in the void,
our values and our freedoms, like old bones, just thrown away,
while evil torched our flag, our dreams, and all we were, destroyed,
then lied in church to push agendas for the power of their stay

We all should stand quite silently and do what we were told
and mask expression so it seems, that only eyes would tell,
for those who preached a brave new world were mining for the gold,
while days that touched the common man, were truly days of hell

They tracked our movements, fed us doctrine, so we would comply,
they rigged the system much like fascists, so they had control
and we became the enemy, whomever sought to fly,
shot down by pawns that started fires, pure chaos was their goal

And I awoke to fevered thought and sweat upon my brow,
I realized no dream but grim reality came with the dawn
and looking back I saw their plans then understood the how,
my fear, we might be more than late and freedom was now, gone

Peace Officers

When chaos reigns and shatters peace,
we look for order through police,
when we need help, when life's askew,
we often call those dressed in blue

When neighbors shared a common street,
there was a cop who walked the beat,
it gave a sense of peace and calm,
where people prayed and played beyond

The road rage now, out of control,
thank GOD we have the State Patrol,
we've lost good men and women too,
some rotten apples, just as true

The chaos in our major towns,
turns children's smiles back into frowns,
it makes the elderly afraid,
society, a failing grade

We take for granted those who serve
and less and less, will have the nerve,
to don the uniform you see,
all underpaid, no dignity

I keep a blue light lit for them
and pray their safe, to an Amen,
I hope when danger comes my way,
the cops are near that darkened day

To Mark the Day

Morning comes and I am here to mark the day,
observations as the hours move along,
I hear songbirds sing their joy from branches all around,
the pleasantry of summer's way,
where youngsters find the time to play
and visions of my past agree,
a child is forever free

A burst of color opens up, on stems that stretch toward sky,
as if to contemplate on life and awed, they open wide
and all they dreamed paints landscapes so,
that we who watch, we too will know,
that there is something greater than,
what stirs the universe and a man,
tis often said, the great I Am

But let us not discuss beliefs,
for dialogue like ships on reefs will all come crashing down
and we are better for the time,
to silence, as a wisdom sign,
for observations taken in,
would bind the earth and man as kin,
while time, in time, it too does pass,
so please enjoy your days, alas,
each morning holds a miracle that's always on the way
and here to mark this given day

As You Mourn

May you know the peace of angels,
when your heart is heavy, vision blurred,
may you comfort in GOD's silence
when you search but there's no word,
may you journey through the valley,
with your loved ones as you mourn,
may you celebrate those taken,
though your heart is sad and torn,
may you cherish times together,
in the memories you share,
only love will guide you through this,
in that love, please know we care

Fathers Away

A reverent prayer for fathers who have left us far behind,
they have passed beyond the veil to a place we cannot find,
but their essence, always heartfelt, never fades from memory
and we honor them, remembering, they are ours, eternally

Better Days

These days I search for solitude,
a hidden place where nature keeps,
unspoiled by the hand of man,
allowed to be alive and free,
a place of the observer's stare,
a place that is for those aware,
of what lies over yonder hill,
a place where freedom finds free will
and still is safe from what men kill,
for fear is no one's friend

Some days I look for quietude,
a state of calm where peace does reign,
a distant hope of the lost man,
who wished a better destiny,
a garden tended with much care,
a place where one can say a prayer,
that better days come to us all,
where man helps man when men do fall
and we respond to help's grave call,
for a much better end

Prayer for Our World

Fly away, fair, white dove, to the place where seldom goes,
a man like me who's searched those spaces few, that no one knows
and tell the angels that I pray the dew is on the leaf,
for as the flora goes, the fauna finds the green relief

Dry seasons take the fat from all who've rested for a while,
it drains the life from all that lives as if the world's on trial,
but you can tell Great Spirit there are innocents who need,
the balance of a healthy earth, for theirs is far from greed

They are the staple of the land, the sea, and air combined,
they cry when man stays so confused, for answers he can't find,
resources dwindle as we move about our tiny globe,
too soon will we remember, how the story went for Job

Fly to tell our maker we're a salty lot at best
but do not give up hope for us through this life's constant test,
please guide our hand to see beyond this day, so we can plan,
a way to bless our planet, for in truth, I know we can

Life Glistens

I guess that I'm most lonesome,
when the hours fade away,
and I am left with one less day to be,
a part of all the wonder,
the little things we often pass,
the ripple on the pond,
the sky and what's beyond,
a smile that makes eyes shine,
a moment shared between two souls,
and one of them is mine

Life glistens when we are aware,
realizing as we go,
it's all around for us to know,
the beauty's always there,
we only need to take the time,
before our time is gone,
to listen closely as we sing,
and be part of the song

A Stranger (An Easter Story)

On my road I met a stranger,
calm, collective was his spirit,
as we greeted one another,
under a gray sky

His eyes cut the surface fabric,
which would hide the deeper subject,
and he asked all things considered,
how was life this day

Something broke within my being,
and I wept as demons left me,
things were not as full of sunshine,
as my face implied

He expressed that mistakes happen,
but the key was in forgiveness,
to oneself as well as others,
as the clouds moved on

Head down, as I wiped my sorrows,
feeling like I'd shed my burden,
stood to thank this astute trekker,
but he disappeared

Nothing but two sandaled footprints,
in the road where he was standing,
indicated I had met him,
this, now sunny day

Song

There are songs of freedom,
songs of love, and hate,
songs to praise our own dear GOD,
which lift and radiate

Songs denote when we were young
and hold our hearts in time,
songs with words and meaning,
either, with or without rhyme

Songs which are without the words
but touch our inner place,
songs which make us laugh out loud
or run tears down our face

But in a world that had no song
I'd trouble with you know,
for without song the birds would hush,
and ears would seldom get a rush,
as songs passed by to get inside,
where those sweet tones all do reside

Sunlight in the Rain

When treatment takes away,
to give life back again,
we often cannot comprehend,
where lies beginnings, to what end

A woman's hair, part signature,
part mystery, part who she is,
lost but never far away,
gone for now, returns someday

She shows her portrait without frame,
it gives us vision to behold,
she is not less for battle scars,
not less for fighting through the pain,
but beauty, sunlight in the rain

A mother, daughter, sister, friend,
all hope, beginnings to an end,
all dream of days when all will see,
the frame around one, cancer free

Two Trees

We're different than long ago,
the bark is chipped and scarred,
the wind has blown our leaves away,
while some grow back another day,
our roots are loosened from the storms,
but days of sun brings that which warms,
the world has turned while time has passed,
we've seen the seasons change,
and through it all our branches touched,
in friendship and in love,
we've stood our ground together,
with GOD's help from above

I'm A Sole Man

Defined by our footwear, we move over earth,
to old age from birth,
with something afoot

The steel–toed shoe of the factory worker,
the orthopedic blacks for diabetics,
the thin–soled satin ballet slipper,
all fit the nature of our role
and cover our steps to meet one's goal

Consider the newborn's soft unmarked pad,
and what will define the young girl or lad

The boot of a military branch,
the sandals of warm climates,
the Italian leather of the well to do,
what kind of a covering applies to you

Recycled tires in a third world place,
heels in New York on 5th Avenue,
western boots in Galveston
or a fashion pair of sneakers on

At the end of the day,
when I look at my ride,
I am thankful they,
are a comfort once they are tried

Led to the Paper

I wrote this piece in pencil,
so, if I made mistakes,
there'd be a way to change the words
and rearrange the thoughts to suit,
simply to eradicate,
by rubbing left and right,
never hard, for paper's thin,
so, one must rub real light,
over choices poorly fit,
into the poem's puzzle space,
but now I find the rubber's gone,
a metal hole stares back at me,
and I am left in panic,
for I find I can't erase,
and therefore, stuck with these few lines
on this restricted space

Breaking Camp at Dawn

Early morning prayer
brings tears again,
as I load the scales
of my life,
measuring the balance,
which keeps me centered,
as chaos tries to tip the see saw
to one side

Great spirit,
guide me through the gauntlet,
that I may find
a gentle stream,
near rolling green
and a seasoned tree,
under which I may rest
for awhile

Transitions

I washed my hands of sorrow,
as joy got in my way,
no misery to borrow,
with happiness that day,
no blues to overcome me,
just smiling heart and eyes,
this was the up to being down,
and much to my surprise!

Look Here

The intricate parts of watching
have filled my empty mind,
it's people, my main interest,
on the move or at the rest,
the art of flesh and bones, I find,
throughout a given day,
while I use up my time
in a look/see sort of way

I don't pretend to have a plan,
I observe all those I can
and get a feel for their life's dance,
some energized, some in a trance,
but through it all I've come to see,
that there are those out there,
who I've caught in a blatant stare,
observing plain old me

The Used Book Store

Two–dollar dreams stacked on the shelves,
each cover held a story
and took me to another place,
from Viking ships to forest elves,
to love or hearts now sorry

Short prose, long novels, briefs and poems,
both health and economics,
religious doctrine had its space,
away from folklore and its gnomes,
plus, Dell and Marvel comics

Old paper scented, red brick store,
with loft that held the classics,
the windows fogged with cobweb lace,
a bell rang to the opened door,
for bookworms and word addicts

I browsed through other people's views,
a journal of their feelings
and often found a piece of me,
between the colors of their news,
the fruit beneath the peelings

The Messenger

The cardinal in vibrant red,
stood tall on bare branched sycamore,
against a robin egg blue sky
and scolded, for the empty feeder

Processing this in my old head,
gave credence to the bird's harsh score,
for February's freeze was nigh
and I had claimed to be the seeder

The aftermath when all was said,
nuts, millet, safflower in store,
I almost heard the feathered sigh,
we thank you, red–winged leader

The Old Neighborhood

Returning to my old hometown I found my neighborhood,
but half the buildings had been razed, much space now void of wood,
no corner store as I remember,
no school bell sounding this September,
very little now remains,
of where a young boy stood

I checked the railroad tracks behind the house where I had grown,
and one set had been taken out which caused me to groan and moan,
some hobo, somewhere, feels my sorrow,
that yesterday is not tomorrow,
seems the watercolors run,
all over time and home

Remembering the trips to church which centered family,
I walked in with a case of sins but left a spirit free,
today, no clergy in the structure,
gone, the candy store and butcher,
everything has changed in time,
with my reality

Though disappointing, I must say it sparked fond memories,
this place where dad came home from work and dropped his set of keys,
where mom was always there for guidance,
regardless rewards or a penance,
sands of time stuck in my shoe,
walked through my mind with ease

The Balancing Act

The odds of getting even,
are as difficult a task,
as making long the short of things,
we fail to achieve,
thus, leaving joy alone
to sadly grieve

The find is always quicker,
than the seeking we all do,
as well as romance is more fun,
than working on the love,
thus, balancing the lows
with the above

The ups and downs, like
elevators, surely are to be,
as permanent as change becomes,
among our daily lives,
thus, giving us repose
along with hives

The end result, beginnings,
is the word which comes to mind,
while clearly, we confuse ourselves,
with journeys we partake,
thus, thinking fast when
we should all brake

Answers

No question goes unanswered,
if the seeker has resolve,
if the quest is undertaken,
there will soon be revelation,
if we pose an inquisition,
soon the truth comes into vision
and those wonders which eluded,
are finally concluded,
to a sigh of understanding,
as the flight makes a safe landing

The Barbershop

Barber pole, red, white, and blue,
lost art, Americana true,
the barber chair, a common seat,
to sit a king or just Joe Street,
a broom and dustpan for the hair,
once part of man now under chair

Conversation for his peers,
among the scissors and shears,
lad's first haircut frightening,
barber takes him under wing,
chairs and benches hug the wall,
as scruffy patrons wait their call

Television, volume low,
gives the wait a little show,
as the barber trims and shapes,
another head cooperates,
shoeshine stand reminds the boys,
this place outlasted all their toys

Neither clip joint nor salon,
he'll trim the excess you've put on,
pleasant ways will bring a smile,
and you'll look good for just awhile,
a tip for those who come his way,
an extra buck or two's OK

Pond and Geese

I watched one dozen geese
land easy on a pond,
wayside for their long enduring trek
and once again I am reminded
of the season's change

How life comes by in chapters,
that we never rearrange,
for in the order that they show,
from spring bud to the white of snow,
we're gifted things,
each season brings,
both in our hands and mind,
from summer's long, hot endless days,
to winter's peace, we find

The sets are taken up and down,
the fresh spring greens,
in autumn, frown,
as they make way for colder days,
and we don on our fleece,
these things all seem to come to me,
as pond accepts these geese

Like Driftwood

A momentary lapse of me,
leaves the vessel floundering at sea,
holes in the sails,
cracks in the mast,
the waters seep,
into a long–journeyed hull,
while the winds hit,
from all points of a compass,
that spins like my mind,
a cork upon the fluid path of life,
guided, I hope,
to the promised land

Personal Pages

I wrote a letter in my youth to future days ahead,
then commenced to do the time to find out what I said,
I traveled years beyond today and watched myself grow old,
I figured, had I listened, I'd have saved time doing what I had been told

I reached a place where we are able, to look back and to see
but could not change a single thing regarding one, small me,
I wept and laughed throughout the viewing, humbled as I look,
to see one's life laid out in years, encompassed in a book

On This Fourth of July

And I dreamed we were wanderers,
amongst the blown-out buildings
we once called home,
smoke smoldered upward from everywhere,
like geysers moving skyward,
carrying our lives, as we knew them, away

We had come to be complacent,
we acted like the Romans
in their final days,
eating grapes while the enemy
took over from within

Now, we are united in our plight,
moving through the motions of shell shock
and disbelief,
as we wonder aloud,
how this could have happened

Then I awoke to reality,
and found my dream
was not too far down the road,
as I prayed for forgiveness,
for letting Freedom rust away

Songbird

A silent mourning came to me
just about midday,
when all was quiet,
almost still,
as I leaned out on my windowsill
and there among the branches green,
hidden well, like a daydream,
a feathered gift who sang her song,
for neither was it right or wrong,
nor too short or ever long,
but pleasant to the ear
and I was blessed for a brief time
to have such music near

Perspective

We look upon towers
as something to climb
and ascend toward the sky,
with articulate eye,
to capture the view,
only feathered eyes do,
realizing how small we are

I wonder of hours,
the passing of time,
as we distance our hearts
with the years and their parts,
to make it untrue,
about death's avenue,
we saw from the tower afar

Unusual Absences

Wary is the night
for day calls,
like a long, lost friend,
hoping to embrace
that which must steal away

When the Student Understands the Teacher

Discovery of wisdom
comes at a cost,
in the scars we acquire
while searching,
as we visit places,
absorbing the faces,
subconsciously
as we go,
learning,
sometimes you drift
or row

A Rusty Bible

Ambiguous feelings
leak from the depths of who I am,
and I find myself
staring down a rusty Bible

Could be the hour to better understand
that which was taught to me,
examining the foundations of beliefs
that I have drifted from,
as a wanderer of time and places

Reminders of death
are bookmarks in between the pages,
days of relative passing's,
shrinking the circle,
of what I knew to what I know,
leaving breadcrumbs for the imagination

Ground feels slick
beneath my feet these days,
and I find, I reach out for stability,
steadying the ship
and gain access to one last port,
if only the weather holds

Power in Prayer

Prayers are like a rose to GOD,
a bouquet in their strength,
believing that prayer for another,
much better than self-centered prayer
but be aware,
whatever you believe,
that prayer will heal when we grieve,
guide us on when we must leave,
mend, if we still have days,
prayer works in mysterious ways

Meditation

A quiet place waits,
when the day is long and tiresome,
when noise surpasses what digests for me
and chaos wants my space,
it is then I find that inner place
where I am one with GOD,
where I am twice restored,
left to continue on with whom I am

The Human Spirit

Most resilient, the human spirit,
that it is tested time and again,
through personal battles,
as well as wars of great scale
and though we are bruised, we heal
and yes, there are losses and so we deal,
we find strength in knowing we share the burden

We pray for guidance, that's for sure,
we pray that science can create a cure,
we're taken back that life's not pure
but through it all our love arises,
spirit under duress resizes
and soon the tunnel dark and dreary,
begins to let us see the light,
then once again, we're given sight

We wring our hands and sigh relief,
to know we've caught the bold, new thief
and joy replaces all our grief,
as we reflect how precious life should be

A Thanksgiving Thought

Predawn thoughts of soldiers
far away from home,
when truth would tell me otherwise,
that peace should be the world's grand prize,
and everyone who ever fought,
should hear the great bell tone,
that we have all begun to see,
we need to find tranquility,
across our Mother Earth,
for we are not some savages
who value not the worth,
of he, who is our neighbor,
he, who is our friend,
he, who is our brother,
or all of this will end
but rather we should reach out,
with an open hand,
together make a stand
and end the petty arguing,
everybody start to sing,
life is a really a lovely thing

By Our Words

I found myself without a friend for something that I said
and though I've said a million things, this one had made me dead,
to her and all her hopes and dreams, for each who had a face,
somehow, I slipped the balance beam and fell out of her grace

As always in my daily life my mouth preceded me,
although I thought I had insight, I guess I could not see,
that one false word had brought me down, a bullet to the brain
and now I mourn a long, dear, friend who shall not come again

Tears

I found a dried tear
and I wondered of its meaning,
had it fallen for life's passing
or the stubbing of a toe,
perhaps it was a tear of joy
it makes me wonder so

I tried to match it to an eye
but it had lost its mass
and now a very thin type skin,
is what remained and dry,
it gave a thinker as myself,
a reason for to sigh

Amazing, all the energy
a tear must hold when new,
it carries laughter and or pain,
from emotions which build up
and need to filter through,
to where one finds that great release,
giving us a bit of peace,
after overwhelming joy
or very painful fears,
we never, ever give much thought
to the purpose of our tears

Find Peace

May we find peace in the face of adversity,
knowing this touches us all,
money and power have zero affect,
for disease has no affiliations or respect
and in a time when nerves are frayed,
may we look within for strength and heart,
to be kind to our neighbors, our fellow man,
whether next door or next nation,
for love is our only station

And like the seasons, this too will pass
but in the interim hope is the key,
which opens the door for both you and me,
lessons are learned on the darkest of days,
teaching us all to perhaps mend our ways,
cherish each other for precious is life,
time will take time, as we move through this strife

On Death

There was a time I feared death for others and myself,
those days in Vietnam, a distant book upon the shelf,
times when I was ill and over thought, wrought visions, dark
and now I look to death, much more a cruise that we embark

The pondering and thinking on the subject drove me mad
and when I lost a friend or family, my inner thoughts were sad,
it made me think about the subject as I tried to sleep
for many times, I heard death's footsteps almost in a creep

And then I realized I was cheating life and all it brings,
so, now I try enjoying everyone and yes, some other things,
oh, death is near I do not doubt, he's silently at bay
but I don't fear for what's in store, he's here to guide my way

Daydreaming Away

Long stretches of the imagination take us to places dreamt of,
when reality displeases the viewer, for lack of joy among the moments
but we might misunderstand where the present lies
and where it will take us, given the patience to stay in view of the next change ahead

We could miss hints of where the compass points to each man's future
and be left wandering aimlessly, where expectations never flower
and our garden lacks, for disillusionment in what is and what is not quite real
still, the daydream gives us time to rest when reality is on overkill

Want and Need

Want and need are diverse roads we travel throughout life
but never do we journey down them both, without some strife,
for each man has to make a choice on which fork they will take
and after all one's needs are met, are wants then a mistake

I'd venture not, for even cavemen must have wished for more,
perhaps a nice cave window in the caveman's own front door,
seems want is more a driver to keep interest very strong,
for life needs varied goals to reach, while we learn right from wrong

There are those who suffer, for they cannot fill their needs,
they are wanting for the parcel but lack for any seeds
and still I'm left to wonder why they serve us so much food,
if you watch fast food commercials, there's so much, it's downright rude

Wasting tons when there are starving souls upon the earth,
makes you sort of wonder if they taunt the poor for dearth
and in the next commercial they will ask with quivered speech,
donations to the starving round the world and out of reach

When we don't feed children adequately in all of our schools,
am often left to wonder who makes up the many rules,
want and need are on the scales of my mind this new morn,
knowing this, begins the crisis of a lethal storm

Answers, I'm not qualified to say just at this time
but an astute observer, all are far from doing fine,
so please help when you're able but don't wave the flag of pride,
your footing might be fine today but later you might slide

Where Will We Be

I wonder of us many souls and where we'll be tomorrow,
if life brings us a day of joy or darker day of sorrow,
if we grow from happenstance or if it's in the plan,
to find our way through many doors unto the great I Am

You'd think that we would be our best before we find our tomb
but we would rather sprinkle salt into each other's wound
and as of late there seems to be a poison in the air,
that lowers our resistance to what is and isn't there

I find the human race to regress, rather than to grow
and I am just as guilty as the next, I would have you know,
but I will try my very best to eradicate my wrongs,
for inside, my heart is broken, for my soul, it truly longs

Search for Kindness

Rather than divide ourselves in two or more,
let us try to find the commonality,
which brings us closer to each other's door,
for in the limitation of our days,
we should search for kindness and its ways,
as time will call us, each one home,
our evidence will then be shone,
as how we spent our days on Earth,
a help or hinderance from birth

Their Last Goodbye

When one soul says their last goodbye,
it brings the rest of us to cry,
for in the days that pass our way,
no hello's will be found to say

We'll recollect good times we had,
we'll smile on, although we're sad,
we'll gather, as a way to show,
our love and strength in letting go

And as the shock begins to wane,
we'll slowly heal from our pain,
time will distance us in time
but loss of loved one, never fine

GOD has promised us a place,
beyond imagination's grace
and knowing that, we rest in peace,
for each of us has our own lease

We're only passing through this way,
on to a loving, brighter, day,
where we will gather once again,
beyond all hurt, beyond all pain

GOD's love will fuel our hungry souls,
we'll understand our loving goals,
we'll shine like stars in the night sky
and those once lost, at hand and nigh

Pen and Paper

The pen and paper are two friends I've left alone too long,
I hear the music and the words but I cannot grasp the song,
an exercise of great frustration comes to visit me,
it seems I've lost the magic, as I worked reality

I see an empty canvas where a scene should just unfold,
perhaps there's nothing more to say, in lieu of growing old,
yet, I'm in hope we can create until our final day,
enlightenment will be our guide and we will know the way

The Wanderer

The distance that lies here to there,
that makes a soul, once lost, aware,
that brings us to reality,
where time moves by eternally

And has us face our storyline,
the vinegar and the sweet wine,
those days we bent the truth we knew,
those timeless shadows that we grew

The tenderness that filled our heart,
when kindness was our work of art,
those sun filled and those rainy days
that marked our trail and our ways

Throughout the timeline that we tilled,
those times we emptied, and we filled,
our coffers as we worked each day,
in what we took or gave away

It seems reflections of our past,
makes us neither first nor last,
but weighs the product of what's sewn
then brings the wanderer back home

The Rich Man

How rich the man who finds his wealth,
in all he sees and hears,
the rivers, lakes, and streams he knows,
cannot be ticketed for worth,
for looking at such miracles,
brings love to soul's rebirth,
the mountains, rolling hills, and plains,
are each a masterpiece,
which artists try to capture
but find they can but only lease
and so, it goes on sunny days,
we all feel much alive,
but rain should get its given due,
for it does nurture me and you

Do fill your senses with our soil
and all it has for you,
remember that the sky's not sad,
because it's colored blue,
appreciate the seasons for,
they're quartered for good reasons,
from winter's rest to spring's rebirth,
to summer's growing season
and on to autumn's harvest,
I think you understand,
the rich are not those looking down,
at what they deem as serf,
but rather those who know land
and waters of our Earth

Wow

Technology,
it frightens me,
an inconvenience I see,
which makes a human quite lazy,
by taking all responsibility,
away from every he and she

It shuts the human factory,
as we have seen with automation,
empty shells across our nation,
no one working at their station

Would have you voice command small chores,
like auto locking your front doors,
it started with one's first remote,
then vacuums that you did not tote,
the strongest muscle, man has now,
are thumbs from texting, hashtag wow!

Virtual trainer speak to me,
for life is lost without thee,
pass the popcorn Alexa, please
or say, GOD bless you, when I sneeze!

For me, I think it's gone too far,
yet infantile, it's who we are
but I can see reality,
where the Terminator comes for thee

My Friend

No words can paint the portrait of my friend,
a part of me that was my song until his end,
our conversations are no more, it's come to me,
we shall not plot nor plan our moves again in this reality

He's gone somewhere far beyond the veiled mist,
where soldiers go towards heaven's gate to reenlist,
where souls all go to wait for those still upon the earth,
I'll miss his love and all he was, remembering his worth

Leaving It All Behind

What portion of greed,
when we leave this place,
what baggage allowed
that transcends our grace,
what good all the gold and silver be,
when man is called to eternity

What tells of the tale
on the dying face,
what defensive move
to explain our case,
what seeds have we sown as legacy,
when we leave the earth, forever free

Be a Light

In dreams, I saw an angel of the Lord
and where I was so deeply angered,
by the darkness in the world,
I was put to ease,
for I was told the truth is gold
and needs be mined from that inner place,
where honesty and love unfold,
with our Savior's endless grace

Find calming peace in GOD's own way,
be clear in all that you might say
and when we reach the end of day,
our message has been one of love

Don't hide from darkness as you live,
don't take when it is right to give,
but be a light, a positive
and when life's low be there, above

For if we take an eye for eye,
if we regress than apt to try,
we'll end up lost beneath GOD's sky,
as crow rather than dove

Walk Softly

Tenderly, we move along life's trail,
for to approach in any other way,
would be cause to miss the finer points
of existence, and the possibility to do good,
leaving past places and encounters,
better than we found them

A Story for Each Soul to Read

I will not judge you for your sins, as GOD will have the time,
I'll not tell you the path to walk, for I do not fill your shoes,
instead, I'll watch my own behavior and hope things turn out fine,
we share this world until we leave and that's the honest news

With respect, I'll live my life and let you all live yours,
it takes true love to make it work for hate's its own disease,
we can live as first born pure, in a land of common shores,
respect and understanding helps bring calm to raging seas

Much truth in knowing stops confusion, as we go,
beneath each cover is a story for each soul to read,
knowing who each other is and what the pages show,
we are here because we are somebody's seed

A Story

In each of us, a story,
a past event that brought us joy or sorrow,
a happening along the way our journey took a turn
and brought us to a place in time where smiles owned the day
or tears became a river for dark hours along the way

We likely all could write a book,
on love and lovers at first look
or when we found what seemed quite lost,
most irreplaceable by cost

We have been hurt beyond the norm,
when trust and honesty are torn,
when highways end up dead end roads
and answers hide in cryptic codes

I'd like to think some telling tales,
of eyeing mice to watching whales,
to valleys we have walked along
or mountains where, one step, we're gone

But as I contemplate my walk,
some tales shan't be told for talk,
would not give justice to be fair,
for one would simply have been there

So, I will end with this insight,
we all move better in the light,
less stumbling, less broken toes,
more time to read of smiles and woes

Smile

Let us cherish our together time,
for it will pass as we move through the veil,
may our moments shared be of good sign
and may we find GOD's love before we pale

May the gift of a passing smile,
warm up your heart in a tender way,
that you share this act with friends a while
and it multiplies throughout each given day

At Last

I am in a better place today,
for someone who had lost their way,
war will start an abscess deep inside the heart,
takes an innocent boy and tears him all apart,

Dark scenes hang heavy in one's mind,
they haunt the soldier, many find,
we medicate to keep them from our door,
but they return another day to haunt us even more

Self–destruction leaves a nasty path,
loved ones hurt from our own rath,
we find, we find our way in later years,
but not without a lengthy trail of tears

I am in a better place today,
as I work to hopefully find my way,
there are scars on my heart to mark the past,
but I'm good with them today, at last

The Journey

Stories in our lives to tell,
some of heaven and some of hell,
we traveled on from mother's womb,
found our music, played our tune

And in our years upon this earth,
found our failures and our worth,
experienced the dead-end road
and longer highways we were sold

Drawn to those who understood,
the knots we find inside the wood,
we're flawed but capable of love,
with some we fit, like hand in glove

Chapters read like poetry,
while others, like the raging sea,
compiled years and aged like wine,
some vinegar, some rather fine

Living, was a long, long test,
to learn about what's truly best,
not always with ourselves in mind,
but thoughtfulness and being kind

I hope I've passed, so far, so good,
this jackass even understood,
that it's about that goodness thing,
not what we take but what we bring

Soul School

We cast our nets toward hope,
for the enduring resilience in men,
so, all need live a decent life,
no matter now or then

We feel it in our hearts,
many actors set the stage,
played, according to our roles,
searching for the missing page

We look within to know,
what's right and wrong, and in between,
we try our best with some unrest,
to try and build a better dream

The Pastor

In the stillness of the dawn as it unfolds, we see,
a lonely pilgrim that could be of you or me,
his curse, to wander on the surface of the earth,
lost from all that's good and holy, near our Savior's birth

As he walks along, he listens for a sign, we say,
as when the clouds break and light chases off the gray,
he knows that there is something that he lacks,
he studies as he goes, in search of ancient tracks

There's a hunger in his soul which needs be fed today,
an empty vessel searching as he makes his way,
stone church ahead where silence is the bated call,
he enters and the mass begins for one and all

Trouble

The trouble with trouble,
is it bursts our own bubble,
it stops up the joy machine
and shuts down that happy dream

It takes center stage,
with its darkness and rage,
it needs to be somehow,
put back in its cage

It disrupts good karma
and shows us life's alley,
we slip from our mountain top,
down to the valley

It darkens our path,
with its unbridled wrath,
but always with fight,
we return to the light

Some lessons are taught,
whether free or they're bought,
whether wanted at all,
we stand, stuck with the ball

I assure you my friend,
that it is not the end
and we work through it all,
never breaking but bend

When we come to the place,
when there's joy on our face,
we have found renewed peace,
from GOD's blessing of grace

A Day at the Beach

Small wonder sits upon the beach sculpting castles in the sand,
while passing onlookers comment on the artist's steady hand,
imagination, a plastic bucket, and shovel, aid this future architect of sorts,
who might in fact decide to make and bake cakes, fruit pies, and yummy torts

A couple covers two large towels as they share each other's eyes,
in love, they do not see beyond themselves for their deep romantic sighs,
their world, a stage where they perform while life goes on around them,
they only know that they were stones and now they are each other's gem

An old man stares out towards the distant waters at the constant waves,
they roll across his two aged feet and wash away those dreams he craves,
he sees the lad engulfed in his creation, remembering his own, long past,
times when he, himself, worked the sand, building a foundation that would last

One woman suns herself in a reclined, green, striped chair, lost inside her mind,
about her job, her looks, the time she's sunned and if a partner she will ever find,
she adds her sunblock just in case, for they say cancer is a constant threat,
adjusts her sunglasses, looks about then returns to her mind when all is set

The rolling waters cast a spell on those souls who ever find this place,
where water meets the edge of sand, where the people come to tan their face,
all are characters in a daytime play, on a long and varied playtime stage,
common in their draw to the ocean's shore, they are written on this sunlit page

Metaphorically Living

If we carried our sins as a bag full of stones,
would they weigh on our hearts even more,
could we take out a stone with a deed of goodwill
or replace it with one, if intentions were ill,
would we burden ourselves until we had our fill,
ending life somewhere down on the floor

If we buried our hates and our hurts like old bones,
would we visit the graves anyway,
as a dear lost companion whom we put to rest,
missing parts of the past that we put to the test
or could life move straight forward, expecting the best,
leaving old things behind for today

If our lives were a number of musical tones,
would the song that we sang bless us all,
notes inspired by attitude, actions, and thought,
melodies we created, we could not have bought,
on the path of our lives that we fervently sought,
would the angels be lifted or fall

I Sat a Time

I walked the forest for a time, then found a stump to sit,
I looked back hard at all my days and wondered where the pieces fit
and then I looked about myself and saw great wonder all around,
the breathing Earth, a living being, in tempo with its own, warm sound

I left those darker days behind and exited the trees
and in the clearing, understood, the vision each man sees,
to have a tranquil life at times, between the trees and field,
to bless humanity than take, without concern of what we yield

All of us Have Worth

At early morning prayers I thought I heard a sound,
it was angelic to my ears, for I heard it all around,
I found myself in thought about the who, what, when, and why,
I looked out past my window to be greeted by the sky

In that early morning hour, I somehow came to know,
how precious life is in all things, that simply come and go,
I've watched the eye of life fade way, to stillness evermore
and wondered on, about what lies beyond that looming door

So now I step quite lightly as I move across the Earth,
I find there's critters underfoot and all of us have worth,
I've crushed a bug or two in spite, when looking back I'd say
but I will further watch my step as I go on my way

The Grateful Pessimist

Here I am again Lord, thankful for another day,
I search for Your infinite wisdom, as I make my way,
I look to answers much as a flower in a seed,
when I understand the moment, I blossom forth, so freed

A better day today, my mantra as I try,
then realize it's me, you see, as sadly I do sigh,
I'll moan and groan my time away, for what I'm cursed to see,
erosion of the human race, a true calamity

Forward

When lost in our importance, it's sad for what we find,
that a humbling correction seems to walk across our mind
then we find our new direction or repeat the same old song,
it's what makes life's days ever short or so very long

The gift of life is always honored by a decent soul,
who takes life's challenges to heart, as their very goal,
instead of digging graveyard holes, at best, for later days,
they're much a novice weaver, as they mend their ways

Sometimes we feel regression but that's life's learning curve,
we manage our direction, knowing when it's time to swerve
and time might share its wisdom, in man's autumn, if you please,
enlightening the forward path as onward each man sees

Moment to Moment

What colors will the day produce, within the chakras of my being,
what path will be my choice in the state of all I'm seeing,
who will I be in contact with throughout the hours coming,
will I be sad from all the crying or happy that I'm humming

What damage will the day incur because of my neglectful ways,
how much have I enhanced the beauty of my given days,
where have I gone, which caused souls on my path such great despair,
was I just a pawn through life, engaged, but never quite aware

As Man Hopes

A mist pours over ground
and silence is the only sound,
a figure finds his knees,
beyond, where there be trees,
where mist meets cloud
and spirit frees,
where truth survives aloud

Polishing the Stone

Trials we endure through life are a test,
if we have the mettle to make us our best
and times when we have all dropped the ball,
another chance comes to our beaconed call

We all start out as sharp stones, in the stream,
but time wears our edges away in life's dream,
where failure attacks, a new challenge occurs,
each step we define, by what's mine and what's yours

Each of us born, owes a debt for our chance,
to better our souls in life's sacred dance,
a lost opportunity never returns,
each one of us gains what each one of us earns

Music Box

The music box holds just one song,
it opens on command,
it will not play the melody
without a given hand

Much like ourselves, we hold a tune,
that plays when we're aligned,
it opens when we feel the love
and share our hearts, I find

And when those hearts all play at once,
a harmony appears,
a choir of humanity
and joy brings man to tears

For all our beauty is within,
the rest is just our shell,
what we create brings out the light,
if truth would know us well

Yet, there are those who will not sing,
their lids are closed it seems,
they gather dust and wane away,
without much hope or dreams

We'd like to hear their special tune
and have them join our song,
for time would always let us know,
the time to move along

The Awakening

Friend and family drop like leaves from my living tree,
moving on to the spirit realm where peace reigns
and love is the norm of each and everyone
but for now, I shall stay with those who remain
and work on loving all, today,
for tomorrow holds the secrets of what will come,
while life's dance moves with music of the hour

Lessons in learning who we were
and who we are today,
are still available to the seekers in this life
and I am but a student of the awakening,
a stone in the stream of existence,
polished over time

www.ingramcontent.com/pod-product-compliance
Lightning Source LLC
LaVergne TN
LVHW050645100826
845148LV00011B/1989

* 9 7 9 8 3 8 5 2 7 2 4 0 2 *